D0324392

Golf: Those Were The Days

Golf: Those Were The Days

Captain William Featherstone-Dawes

PORTICO

First published in the United Kingdom in 2011 by
Portico Books
10 Southcombe Street
London
W14 0RA

An imprint of Anova Books Company Ltd

Copyright © Anova Books 2011

All rights reserved. No part of this publication may be
reproduced, stored in a retrieval system, or transmitted
in any form or by any means electronic, mechanical,
photocopying, recording or otherwise, without the prior
written permission of the copyright owner.

ISBN 13: 978-1-907554-43-8

A CIP catalogue record for this book is available from
the British Library.

10 9 8 7 6 5 4 3 2 1

Reproduction by Rival Colour Ltd.
Printed in China by Everbest Printing Co Ltd

This book can be ordered direct from the publisher.
Contact the marketing department, but try your bookshop first.

www.anovabooks.com

CONTENTS

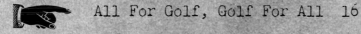

THE AULD DAYS OF GOLF.

 What have we here? This collection of roadside gents look like they have some villainy in mind. Hard to believe but these assorted footpads are the finest golfers in the land about to venture out on a swift round of the old course at <u>Leith</u>.

With only one club apiece they won't be wasting time on club selection and they'll scoot round 18 holes quicker than you can say, "hoots mon, out of me way, hoo d'you think ye are?"

As the price of golf clubs tumbled from four guineas to three guineas four shillings and threepence, so the keen golfer acquired more than one club. The smiling fellow in the centre of this photo is laden with a positive arsenal of clubs; a spoon, a brassy, a mashie niblick, a driving spooter, a bobbling cleek, a wee dredgie and many others with names straight out of a Rabbie Burns poem.

———◦———

All watch as Mr. Henry McAllister, the well-known bootmaker of Troon, addresses his gutta percha ball on the first tee.

Don't let those Dutch fellows claim it was their invention! Golf is as Scottish as tartan and the Loch Ness Monster. And don't just take our word for it, King James II banned the playing of football and golf in 1457 because he wanted his archers out practising - shooting Englishmen not birdies!

So here we are on the hallowed turf of St. Andrews, the rightful home of golf and what a crowd to celebrate the opening day of the 1876 golf season. Those were the days when a chap could play 18 holes in a top hat or bowler and still be dressed appropriately to sit down to dinner with the Queen. Not that she liked golf over much.

The moustaches say it all, these five chaps are Edwardian through and through. They have Edwardian Plus Twos, Edwardian caps, and finely trimmed, waxed Edwardian moustaches. Seen here on a misty autumn morning on the fourth hole at Stoke Poges these lads will soon be off to fight in the Great War, the war to end all wars. Such a pity they couldn't invent the golf bag before they went.

☞ Did someone say polish the spoons? It's no surprise that the fairer sex rush to the golf links when they know cutlery is involved.

That's a baffing spoon in Dorothy Campbell's lovely hands.

Miss Campbell is a marvel at the sport and likes nothing better than to spank a feathery on a windy afternoon. No surprise that she has invested in the patented Weighted Cap Stabilisation Aid For Ladies to keep her from blowing off.

ALL FOR GOLF - GOLF FOR ALL

Fore! Or should that be Ahoy There! Look at this merry crowd enjoying the latest craze of the time - midget golf - golf so small you can play it aboard a ship! The Cunard line have installed this nine-hole miniaturised course on their cruising steamer 'Atlantis'.

In our photograph, Miss Tunstall aims to pop her ball past Horatio Nelson gazing down on the Trafalgar Square hole. If she's not too careful where she's swinging, she could have his other eye out!

More **midget golf** on the ocean waves. Some young buck tries the Grand Old Duke of York's hole. He can march it up to the top of the hill, but it might just march back down again. Here's a thing you don't often see on a regular golf course - lovers playing a round with their sweethearts.

These **newly-weds** on the voyage from Southampton to New York are tackling midget golf in the calm waters of the English channel. It might not be so easy in the choppy waters that lie ahead. A metaphor for marriage itself perhaps.

Anything you can do, we can do better. When it comes to a bigger, brasher midget golf course, those damn yanks won't be beaten.

———⟫◦⟪———

This midget course in the centre of New York City takes up a city block but allows workers to swap their purchase ledgers for putters during luncheon.

———⟫◦⟪———

Budding Walter Hagens and Bobby Joneses can tackle the delights of the East Course or the West Course. Mickey Mouse? You bet your bottom dollar!

Talk about clocking on and clocking off - how about clocking golf? This adorable creature - Miss Lucyenne Herval-Smith, aged 19 - likes to relax at home with her own putting green upon which has been marked out the dial of a clock.

The hole is at the centre of the dial and players take putts from each position of the clock.

Looks like this flapper isn't getting in a flap about her perfect putting stance.

Don't put your **daughter** on the stage Mrs Worthington - especially if her backswing ties her up in knots.

A novel teaching scheme is put in action at the Finchley Golf Club.

———◆◇◆———

With half of the new membership never having swung a club in their lives, professional Mr. Dalby has arranged lectures in the club lounge.

———◆◇◆———

For a **shilling** a head Mr. Dalby delivers hints and tips on grip, posture and swing in front of an attentive audience. But did he finish with a song on that old Joanna...?

Perhaps a recreation of when Charles II took his courtiers 'upon the golfe grounds' you muse?

Not a bit of it, actually. These quaintly dressed folk are being schooled in the rudiments of the game by the professionals at Clacton-on-Sea as a publicity stunt to get more people learning the game.

And as history recalls, that comely Nell Gwynne was game for anything.

"Show me a golfer at 17 and I'll show you the man,"
reads the Jesuit motto (if you add 10 to the figure
and substitute the word "golfer" for "boy"). These lads
from Tiffin School in Kingston-upon-Thames are well
used to learning by rote, so what better way to teach
them golf than in rote-ation, at Home Park Golf Course.

Knocking lumps out of the turf on a bright spring
afternoon is a lot better than triple algebra -
I'll say.

...and what is sauce for the goose is also sauce for the gander.

<hr/>

Which ardent schoolboy wouldn't want a gander at this sextet of American high-school gals in their skimpy gym attire?

<hr/>

 Looks like their teacher is taking no risks and stands well back from the firing line. Future-ologists have predicted that in ten years' time, men and women will be competing in the same golf tournaments.

Back in dear old Blighty our ladies sport the
smartly tailored look with skirts and belted
cardigans.

Young and old, our ladies embrace the game and take
immense pleasure in it. Look at those two dear old
sticks at the back, straight out of casting for
The Lavender Hill Mob they are, but come rain
or shine you'll find them out on the ladies' tees giving
it a solid whack with a mud-encrusted brassy. More power
to your elbow gran and maybe lift that elbow
a little higher, too.

We've all heard about the 19th hole, but golf lessons in the bar? This is surely taking things too far! A chap likes to enjoy his Mackeson and the chance to recount terrific shots he made on his round without another chap having a bally lesson only feet away.

***

Things are not what they seem. This is the bar of the Starcross Hotel run by Mr. Bob Midwood, the well-known Barnsley hotel keeper. Every Tuesday is golf club night and patrons can enjoy a bottled or cask ale while learning more about the sport they all follow. Fore! in the car park there!

 Not to be outdone, the ladies of <u>Oakdale Swimming Club</u>, Florida, also combine swimming training - or, as it's known Stateside, 'swim training' - with their love of golf.

Before these water babies take to their Olympic-sized pool they loosen up their muscles with a spot of driving, tutored by the luckiest fellow in Florida, Mr. Wallace T. Spirling III.

Now then chaps, that's what I call a water hazard!

And as for these native ladies in Hawaii there's no way they could set foot on a British golf course dressed like that!

———◆◆◆———

It would most certainly give the secretary of any Home Counties' golf course a heart attack.

Wool, cotton or tweed skirts, yes. Grass, no, no, no.

TAKING THE GAME TO
JOHNNY FOREIGNER

"What's this," you say, "have Wilson, Keppel and Betty
dropped their famous sand dance and opted to play golf?"
No. Betty would not be allowed to appear on the course
in her vaudeville attire.

The Great British Empire colonized the world and now
it is attempting to civilize Johnny Foreigner by
teaching him the superior game of golf. In this instance
by asking him to build a course and then to carry his
clubs. This vagrant donkey herder muses,
'Hmmm, Mustafah game of golf some time.'

Once a chap picks up a club, he is hooked, whether he comes from St. Andrews or Sapporo. His traditional robes may allow this stocky Japanese gent to swing freely, but that wooden footwear is not going to give him suitable purchase upon the turf.

———◦———

See how his pretty wife frowns. Golf widows are the same the world over. He is spending too much time engaged in sporting activity. She needs to nip this one in the flowering cherry bud.

Ah, the indomitable spirit of the Yankee gal. Our American cousins, with thousands of acres of God's Own Country at their disposal weren't slow to convert them to the pleasures of golf. As many know, each Yankee state has its own curious set of laws, byelaws and regulations regarding the wearing of hats, the spitting of tobacco and the skinning of raccoons in public

places. In the state of <u>Vermont</u> it is illegal for women
to use fairways and must play all their golf from a
stream edge. With all the pioneer pluck that carved out
this formidable country they won't be put off. Male
members have remarked that even given full use of the
fairways they would most likely end up there anyway.

The **fashions** may not be up to date in Kansas City
but these are gals who can't say no to a morning of
golf, once the bright golden haze of the meadow has
burnt away.

———————>∘<———————

What was once farmland is now used to grow golf club
memberships proving, if proof were needed, that
the farmer and the groundsman can be friends.

Hold up there Yankee Doodle- who put that rug on the twelfth green? Why, that rug is the twelfth green. Such is the clamour to take part in the game of golf, even areas which cannot sustain adequate lawn grass have been employed to cater for the rampant demand, with rugs used for the putting surface.

Luckily for our American chums they are blessed with serious-minded students at their universities.

Should such a prospect behold some **rugger-playing British undergraduates** out for larks, one can imagine all 18 'greens' ending up on the women's dormitory roof.

Why have these chaps taken their shirts off, did they find a hole in one? Perhaps they were betting on the outcome of the contest and lost their shirts. Most players of the game get hot under the collar at some point in their round, but removing one's shirt is not the mark of a gentleman.

———◆———

A friendly word from the secretary will soon put them right and avoid unpleasantness in the future. Left unchecked this kind of attitude will lead to social decay and one could even find a taxi driver or a builder playing next to one on the course. So our advice to you chaps is - Keep your shirt on.

Oh misery me! Have we turned up at a wake?
These gloomsters look terribly downhearted. Is the
fellow in the centre holding an urn with the ashes
of old Bunty Fotheringham, last of the class of 1867 who
died of a heart attack when he finally cracked 100? No.

The man on the left clutching a smoke is the celebrated
American golfer Walter Hagen. The man holding the
trophy is Mr. Samuel Ryder who is the sponsor of the
new competition between Britain and America to determine
how much better the British golfers are.

The chap on the right is the captain of the British
team Mr. George Duncan. If Mr. Duncan is
unsuccessful in his quest then a career in
undertaking surely beckons.

RadioService

Out on the course and battle commences. No guesses as to which side of the Atlantic this particular fixture is being played, with forecaddies dressed up in overcoats and mitts as though equipped for polar exploration. It's almost May on the Moortown Golf Club but it is hard to tell.

One might even think it was the middle of the Antarctic winter. One advantage for the British side in these inclement conditions is that the famous explorer Captain Robert Scott was a Briton. The disadvantage? He never made it back to the clubhouse.

As the great Shakespeare wrote, "All's Well That Ends As You Like It". Mr Samuel Ryder hands over the trophy to the victorious Mr. George Duncan in a moment of sheer euphoria for the British side.

Mr Duncan's cup may be overflowing but his traditional stiff upper lip prevents him from breaking into a smile. We are certain that once the cameras are put away he will be performing cartwheels down the fairway.

"Hello, is that Sandwich 291? I have a call for you." Those are the words we could have plucked from the mouth of this delightful young lady sat at her telephone exchange. But look a little closer - this is the latest piece of equipment used by the BBC's Home Service to report on important golf matches.

With exciting developments in the field of radiogram engineering, the science boffins have designed a battery small enough to fit inside the back of this portable commentary station. Henry Longhurst may well know what the 19th hole looks like, but now he has the chance to acquaint himself with the other 18.

What will they think of next? Not to be outdone, those go-ahead Americans have trumped our Outdoor Portable Reporting Station with their own Rapidly Mobile Outdoor Portable Reporting Station. This Heath Robinson contraption looks like it was designed for Mrs Mopp to hang out the washing on, but the large aerial loop enables reporters to swiftly follow matches from hole to hole while maintaining a constant and reliable commentary. Careful not to beep that horn at a crucial moment old boy!

LADIES' DAY

Once a week the first tee is reserved for the ladies of the club and what a grand addition they have made to the game.

———◆◇◆———

Many, such as Mrs Parkinson, put their heart and soul into each and every stroke. With nostrils flaring and teeth gnashing one can imagine that Queen Boadicea of the Iceni tribe would take to golf in just such a fashion. Fore left!

Each and every hole an adventure, especially at beautiful <u>Machrihanish in Argyll and Bute</u> where one must drive across the Atlantic to reach the first fairway.

Here **Miss McConachie** has found a good lie on the sands after hooking her tee shot towards the sea. With no out of bounds on the left there is an ocean of space to land one's ball at low tide, providing one doesn't disappear down a crab hole or end up in a rocky pool.

One might have a deal of a job explaining to the Rules Committee that the Atlantic Ocean was casual water.

Everything but the kitchen sink! These two gal pals are heading off for a weekend of golf and it looks like they have remembered everything. The bitch at the front is even equipped with her own set of goggles.

—◆—

Most importantly they have remembered to take the kettle along for a refreshing brew up whenever they require it. Tea, golf and your most favourite gal pal - a weekend to savour.

When you've rattled off some stirring shots over the
Old Course what better way to celebrate, than with
a relaxing smoke.

◆━━◆━◆━◆━━◆

This pretty young thing is enjoying an Eve,
'the first truly feminine cigarette, almost as pretty
as you are' or so the advertising copy tells us.
Who are we to disagree.

'These two gal pals indulge in a spot of friendly banter before taking to the course at the Findlay's Embrocation Northern Foursomes at Moor Park.

The lady on the right looks a **trifle frosty.** Perhaps her beefy chum has received a compliment from an admiring male member and she hasn't?

Or perhaps she is dashed annoyed at not being able to purchase a swift toddy before teeing off. Ladies are not allowed to buy their own drinks at British golf courses.

That **and** the vote in the same century would have been too much to countenance.

Flaming June? Flaming marvellous we say.
But a spot of rain isn't going to put off these
pretty young creatures as they tee off together
at Moortown.

Stuffy old dyed-in-the-wool majors may complain
that having ladies on the course is a distraction
and only inflames the passions of hot-blooded males,
but my word, it's a small price to pay.

Here we are at Ranelagh for the Ladies' Golf Union spring meeting. Mrs Pearson on the left and Miss Dawkins on the right. Miss Dawkins is a prodigious talent and can drive the ball almost as far as a man. Her solid stance and broad shoulders help her achieve extraordinary distances with a variety of cleeks and woods and she is undefeated in the last 12 tournaments. She is very much the envy of her fellow competitors.

Watch the birdie! Why, we're about to see the
birdies and pars, and, with a fair wind and a following
sea, maybe a few eagles too.

———◦———

These ladies, including the redoubtable Miss Dawkins,
are competing at <u>Alwoodley Golf Club</u>. This first round
matchplay tie also features the lovely Miss Lobett
(far right) whom we first saw at Moortown. The match,
of course, is a fourball.

Keeping warm might be the order of the day back in blustery Blighty, but in the southern state of Georgia these showgirls simply want to cool off.

<hr />

A combination of good approach play has left all four girls with the chance of a single putt on a green that shows few challenges. No need to attend the flag Betty-Sue, they can all see the line from where they are.

Ah, that's more like it. A handily placed ice block at the edge of the green effects two solutions. The chance of a sit-down between holes combined with a cooling remedy for the aching limbs. But what one really needs at times like this is a refreshing drink.

Iced tee anyone...?

WIZARD INVENTIONS

Where would golf be without its backroom boys? These days the development of top notch equipment is big business and everyone wants a slice of the pie. To give your golf equipment the edge, whether it be the perfect ball or perfect driver, one needs to call in the backroom boys. They said no to hickory shafts and out hickory shafts went. They said no to leather grips and out leather grips jolly well went. With their help, balls bounce further and clubs hit the ball longer. Industry boffins predict that a 275-yard drive may soon be possible with the latest equipment.

Talk about coming up short on the green! This 18-inch putter is no novelty item, it is perfectly legal and adheres to all the rules set down by the Royal and Ancient Golf Club.

It was used in the Open at Sandwich by American professional Joshua Crane who swears by it. There are certainly no complaints from his caddie, Billy McNeill, who is a great admirer of Mr. Crane's short game.

<hr />

However, when taking a drop of two club lengths, you can bet that Billy doesn't reach for the putter!

All quiet on the Western Front? That's the western front of the fifth hole at Moore Place, Esher.

Instead of the traditional bell, rung to let one's fellow golfers know the fairway is clear, the golfers behind can snoop over the hill with a novel golfing periscope.

It saves a 100-yard hike up the fairway to check all is clear in front. In 20 years' time all golf courses will be equipped with radar to achieve this function.

RADIO SERVICE

It don't mean a thing if you ain't got that swing! Or so Duke Ellington told us. This devilish-looking **contraption** installed by Mr. Lillywhite at his Knightsbridge premises claims to give users a faultless swing. And that's no jive. Jive being the swing-speak word for foolish talk.

———◦———

Expect more **hep cats** to be making their way to Mr. Lillywhite's store to get in the groove and improve their swing. It is out of sight.

Swing a little rusty? Why not take a lesson with the robot golfer; he has a perfect swing every time. Using a lever at the back, beginners can slow down the swing action of our mechanical chap to see exactly what does what, and what goes where and when.

By the look of him, he's a raffish fellow, the kind often seen propping up the bar at the 19th hole and keen to buy a lady a drink. Luckily for his two young protégés he has no casters on his stand and could not be wheeled into the clubhouse and possibly has no money either.

HENRY ON THE EIGHTH

'These smart and amiable-looking lads appear to be waiting for 6d for their caddying duties. Not a bit of it. These are the famous Cotton brothers, Leslie and Henry, of the Alleyn's School, Dulwich. Young Henry, on the right, was so ticked off at being made to carry the prefects' cricket kit home on the bus that he gave up the game of cricket and started playing golf. In no time at all he has become expert at the game. So it's a big thank-you to the Alleyn's prefects for giving us a future Open champion with their dirty laundry.

'The right crowd, but no crowding', the famous Brooklands slogan, could be applied to the society set following the young Henry Cotton around <u>Gleneagles.</u> Smart dress is indeed the order of the day with smartly turned-out spectators following the matchplay in close attendance.

———⋙◆⋘———

For the gents, gone are the bowlers and toppers of old, replaced by the ubiquitous tweed cap. Tossing one gayly in the air to celebrate a splendid victory is less common these days as spectators lacking headgear are obliged to return to the clubhouse.

What a crazy world of fashion we live in.
Ten years on and there's hardly a cap to be seen amongst
the gallery of spectators lining the fairways of
Royal St. George's, Sandwich.

Henry Cotton strides purposefully down the first fairway
accompanied by his wife, the lovely "Toots" Cotton. The
fearsome Mrs. C will brook no criticism of her husband -
see how her eyes scan the crowd with a fearsome purpose
after a casual remark aimed at Henry's opening drive.

We're glad to say that Henry went on to score a
memorable victory assisted, of course, by the
lovely Toots.

Watch out, Jerry, this man is deadly accurate from 200 yards.

Airman Cotton has signed up to serve king and country
with the Royal Air Force. There's no likelihood Henry
will be sent off for frontline duties with his Lee
Enfield rifle, but should the opportunity arise then
he'll be more than glad to send Jerry into the nearest
bunker. With no relief.

LIVESTOCK ON THE COURSE

What's the difference between a chicken and a golfer? One likes to scratch and one likes to play off scratch. These chickens are cooped up at Surrey's West Hill Golf Club, an initiative dreamt up by a Mr. Claude Harris. As part of the Dig for Victory campaign Mr. Harris has persuaded the club to devote space between the first tee and third green for laying hens. Long-established golf clubs are just like chicken coops in that they have their own noted pecking order, with the Captain ruling the roost. Except the really bad golfers don't have their necks wrung if they fail to perform!

Aiming for a birdie! Mrs Carpenter of Tring chips a shot over these geese that have taken residence on the course at Ranelagh.

A golf course represents home from home for these noisy wildfowl; they have a lake to swim in, fairways to graze and then there are these curious people who pass by waving sticks at white eggs they really should be incubating.

No sooner has the egg come to rest than the dashed human comes along and bashes it with a stick again. Ooops, there goes another one!

If it's not geese on the fairway it's sheep. But you will hear no complaints from golfers at Mill Hill Golf Club about sharing their facilities with some woolly companions.

With this herd of Suffolks in residence the rough has never been shorter and the lies never been better. The odd spot of sheep business on the shoes is a small price to pay for an extra 20 yards off the tee peg.

Well, blow me! If this isn't the prettiest herd of fillies ever let loose on a golf course.

These members of the Women's League of Health and Beauty use the wide open spaces of the Missenden Valley Golf Course to demonstrate the loveliness of the female form in a dance dedicated to Aphrodite, goddess of female beauty.

Very sensibly, these girls have taken their shoes off.

Two loyal servants attend Miss Runnacles as she drives off the fifth tee at Surbiton. They are her chauffeur Mr. Wakeman and 'Barney' the dog.

———◆◇◆———

Equipped with a rudimentary harness to attach the golf bag, Barney acts as caddie for the round. He may perform an adequate job of transporting the clubs around 18 holes, but his skills really come into their own when the ball disappears into the rough. 'Hmm,' he is thinking, 'that's a particularly grand drive from my mistress.'

'Bruce' of <u>Pinner Hill</u> does a similar job for Mrs Hamilton. The pedigree Alsatian has been equipped with an ingenious harness that allows him to pull the most modern of accessories, the golf trolley. Bruce likes all kinds of holes; long par-fives, short par-threes, but his particular favourite is the dog-leg.

Pity the poor bunny if Mrs Hamilton's ball should disappear down a rabbit hole and find Bruce's great German snout pointing down at him.

This little chap is in a spot of bother, so it's lucky
that Fido is nearby to give him a helping hand.
Or should that be paw?

———————⟫•◦•⟪———————

We admire the courage and tenacity of this small fellow,
but an adult should be sorting out what is a very
risky position.

———————⟫•◦•⟪———————

Taking a wooden club from a water hazard is a poor
choice of shot and will likely result in further dropped
strokes. Not to mention some very wet plus-fours.

If you can't get a dog, why not get a donkcy to do the donkey work. Neddy is 60 years old, but he's still keen to head out onto the golf course with his charming mistress Miss Margery Waddell.

Margery informs us that it is a carrot and stick arrangement; Neddy carries the sticks, and then he gets the carrot. Simple as that.

If you can't get a dog or a donkey why not call up the circus and hire a little elephant.

Carrying a bag of clubs is nothing for the humorously named Tiny who could carry several bags or indeed a mixed foursome on his back if required.

But should the baby elephant fail to follow etiquette and walk across the putting green then he'll be leaving the greenkeeper the biggest pitchmarks in the world to repair. You could say a jumbo-sized problem.

Here's one professional golfer who's happy to accompany a rabbit out on the golf course. For Mr. Tom Burrell from the Bushey Hall Golf Club loves nothing better than to practise his drives along with his pet rabbit "Niblick".

———◆◇◆———

Two-year-old Niblick likes to watch proceedings from the safety of the tee box. Mr. Burrell believes the animal brings him good luck, but Niblick's good fortune is that his owner prefers two lucky rabbit's feet, to just the one on his watch fob.

GOLFING LARKS

What a hilarious chap that Mr. Buster Keaton is. He and professional golfer Mr. Gene Sarazen are larking around on the practice grounds in Monterey, yet still his face remains impressively deadpan despite a brassy around the gills. The well-known Hollywood star may have known exactly where to stand in Steamboat Bill Junior to escape the falling house, but common sense seems to have deserted him on the golf course. After a stern talking-to about the niceties of golf etiquette, we're certain Mr. Sarazen will put Buster firmly in the picture.

This **snappily-dressed** chap looks like he knows
his way round a golf swing. Why it's that most elegant
of fellows Mr. Walter Hagen, and with the dome of
St. Paul's in the background and Waterloo Bridge below,
we can triangulate that he must be standing upon the
roof of the Savoy Hotel.

Mr. Hagen is over here to press the claims for
professional golf at the Open Championship in Kent.
He may not be allowed in the clubhouse at Royal
St. George's after renouncing his amateur status,
but he can stay in the best hotel in the country.
What's more, they seem to have let him up to the
roof to practise. That's one in the eye for you,
Mr. Secretary of Royal St. George's.

Her name is Peg, don't you know. Tee Peg. This beautiful young lady is placing all her trust and her chances of a good marriage in the driving skills of Mr. Jack Redmond, the world champion trick golfer.

Mr. Redmond is about to hit a golf ball from the roof of the 26-story Victoria Hotel in New York City in a stunt organised to promote the new midget golf course the hotel has installed upon the roof. The young lady lying perfectly still is Miss Silvia R. Jucherinar. She is Mr. Redmond's 14th assistant.

Back on terra firma, this trio of lovely ladies are contriving a golf tableau to catch the eye. The sole of one's shoe is a far more sensible place to tee off a ball than the forehead, but the roof of a motor vehicle is hardly the ideal teeing ground.

———✦———

It is no matter. These diversions are simply intended to stimulate the eye in a new advertisement for the latest model from the Lincoln Motor Company. They hope to attract men keen on the pleasures of golf by placing the two in association.

The pleasures of female company need no advertisement.

'T'hose barmy Yanks, what will they do next? This madcap fellow is attempting to drive a golf ball from the uppermost wing of a biplane. He is not connected to the plane in any fashion, yet he has struggled up there laden with driver and golf bag.

Mr. Al Wilson maintains his balance by jamming one foot in front of the forward wing strut and the other hard against the rear strut. The ball is attached to the wing by glue, but could dislodge at a moment's notice.

Should Mr. Wilson himself dislodge it would be a far more perilous matter. Now that really is what one could call an air shot.

These two tribal chiefs have long since smoked the pipe of peace, but now they battle it out on the golf course instead. Brown Buffalo aims a bow and arrow upon which he has impaled a golf ball. Waiting his turn is Sitting Eagle and his son Little Sitting Eagle who will use golf clubs.

Brown Buffalo has big reservations about using golf clubs and prefers his traditional native weapon, but Sitting Eagle is a dab hand with the Scottish implements and has gained many scalps in matchplay competition.

After a thoroughly pleasant round at the Washington State course they join their wives Mrs Brown Buffalo and Mrs Sitting Eagle for a heap big pow wow at the club wigwam.

You would think the odd golfball on the nut was an acceptable occupational hazard for most caddies. They are generally speaking not the brightest of fellows, for whom a blow on the head might be a welcome stimulus. But a new innovation from the Accrington Ironwork Company has made their job a degree safer.

———◦———

The Go-Anywhere Caddy Protector allows a caddy to venture out onto the practice ground to retrieve balls without fear of a pummelling from other golfers' balls. It can also be used on the course when caddying for rich children or senior ladies.

Mercy me, have these chaps lost their senses?
Golf may drive a chap to drink, ruin his
friendships, wreck his marriage and drain his
pocket but what madness drives a fellow to
public indecency?

These chaps must surely be Australians!

THE LEADER BOARD

'T'hey say horse racing is the sport of kings, well then, golf must be the sport of leaders. The bulky frame of President Taft commands the first tee and it looks like it's his honour. **'Big Bill'** is the first U.S. president to openly admit his affection for golf despite fears from advisors that it will alienate Americans who regard it as a rich man's game. This political heavyweight may know much about scoring political points on Capitol Hill, but during one round at Bar Harbor in Maine he notched up a magnificent score of 27. Sad to say this singular feat was achieved on the 17th hole alone.

A game for the people indeed. Bearded and bespectacled Cuban leader Fidel Castro tries his hand at a tee shot at the Havana Country Club.

The feared revolutionary, who will not contemplate any form of opposition, is always guaranteed to win every competition he enters - whether he returns in 45 or 95. He leaves it up to his many aides to fidel the scorecard. Come to think of it, an outspoken, golf-loving, cigar-smoking politician reminds one of...

Golf must be a frustrating pastime for Winston Churchill. Never one to contemplate occupying the left or centre ground, all his shots must end up out on the right.

After this particular baffy shot went clattering into the trees, the great man was heard to mutter that it was a diabolical game sent to torment its adherents - but still time better spent than an afternoon with Stanley Baldwin.

Who's that astride a muddy cairn? Why it is none other than music hall comedian and band leader Mr. Harry Lauder, described by Mr. Churchill as "Scotland's greatest ever ambassador" and famed for his Scottishness.

"It is very sad the way the Scottish atmosphere has gone out of the game," wrote author P. G. Wodehouse.

"In my youth one took it for granted that to be a good golfer you had to be Scottish, preferably with a name like Sandy McHoots or Jock Auchtermuchty."

Mr Lauder is attempting a tricky approach, teetering on the cairn with his spade-mashie. Good luck to you, sir, and keep right on to the end of the road.

PHOTOGRAPH ACCREDITATION

We are most obliged to the following photographic bureaus for their assistance in providing images of the highest quality for this work. In particular to Mr. Luigi Di Dio of the Getty Archives of Maida Vale, London, who furnished us with black and white photographs for the following pages: 17, 21, 22, 25, 26, 28, 31, 32, 35, 42, 53, 54, 56, 63, 65, 66, 68, 71, 72, 74, 76, 85, 88, 91, 93, 95, 97, 98, 99, 101, 103, 108, 109, 113, 114, 118, 123.

Thanks also to Mr. John Moelwyn-Hughes of Corbis Images, a firm residing in Queen's Park, London, who furnished us with plates for the following pages: 9, 11, 12, 14, 18, 36, 38, 41, 44, 45, 51, 59, 60, 86, 104, 106, 121, 124, 127, 129, 131, 133, 134, 138, 143, 144.

We are also most grateful to the Library of Congress photographic archives of Washington, D.C., United States of America, for providing us with the photographs on pages: 7, 46, 49, 78, 79, 80, 83, 116, 137.

Photographic research: Evan Joseph

Design: Claire Marshall

Layout: Sarah Rock